A Cookie Trail

Written by Jane Kelley

Illustrated by Frank Farrar

Characters

Maggie	**Peter**
Micky	**Carly**
Ling	**Sam**

Setting: the school playground

Maggie: Can you see anyone? Ling said we would all meet here after school.

Micky: No. I don't see them anywhere.

Ling: Hey, Micky! Maggie! We're in the playhouse!

Maggie: Hi! Is there room for us?

Peter: Not really. There are four of us in here already.

Micky: But there are four walls and two seats on each wall.

Maggie: Yeah – that makes eight seats. There are only six of us, including Micky and me.

Carly: But our backpacks take up one seat each.

Ling: Oh, come on, everyone! Maggie and Micky can squeeze in. Let's pile our backpacks together.

Peter:	But six backpacks won't fit on one seat.
Ling:	We only need to clear off two seats. I can put my backpack next to Carly's. Sam can put his next to Peter's.
Sam:	Okay. Maggie can sit by you. Micky can sit by me.
Ling:	What about their backpacks? I mean, I can hold my backpack in my lap.
Micky:	Me, too. I have some peanut butter cookies in mine.
Peter:	Why didn't you say so? Come on in!
Carly:	Okay then, but only if you're going to share.
Peter:	How many cookies do you have?
Micky:	Nine.

Sam: Oh. That won't come out even.

Maggie: We can have one each. That leaves three.

Sam: I think Micky should get two cookies. He brought them.

Maggie: Wait a minute. Three is **half** of six.

Micky: Yeah, we can break the three extra cookies in half to make six halves. Then we can have one and a half cookies each.

Carly: Ling can break the cookies. She's the most careful.

Peter: Yeah. I don't want my half to be more like a **fourth**!

Ling: Okay, but let's go out and play first. Then we'll be hungrier and the cookies will taste better.

Sam: Good idea. Let's meet back here in ten minutes.

Maggie: I'll race you to the basketball court, Micky!

Micky: That's not fair! You got a head start. . .

Ten minutes later

Sam: Now I am hungry. Where are those cookies, Micky?

Micky: They're right... Wait a minute! They're gone!

Carly: Someone must have taken them.

Ling: Only we knew where they were, so it must have been one of us. Come on, who did it?

Everyone: I didn't take them!

Micky: Let's figure out who the **thief** is.

Ling: How?

Micky: Well, I was playing basketball with Maggie the whole time.

Maggie: Yeah, that's true.

Ling: That **rules out** you two. And I was with Sam on the swings, so we didn't do it.

Sam: Only Peter and Carly were alone.

Maggie: What were you two doing? We can **time** how long it took you. Then we'll know who had time to sneak back here and take the cookies.

Micky: Maggie loves showing off her new watch!

Peter: Well, I went over to the school so I could use the bathroom. Then I asked Ms. Stein for an energy bar. I still have the wrapper here.

Ling: An energy bar? But we were going to have cookies in a few minutes!

Peter: I know, but I was already hungry! Anyway, do you want to time me or not? I have nothing to hide.

Sam: Well, it takes four minutes to get to the bathrooms, and that's if you're fast.

Carly: That makes eight minutes there and back.

Sam: And Ms. Stein can take two minutes to find the right snack.

Micky: Eight plus two is ten minutes. I guess Peter didn't do it.

Peter: I told you I didn't!

Carly: My turn. First, I was on the monkey bars with those kids over there.

Maggie: Let's time how long it takes to get there. Ready, set, go!

Micky: Okay, that was ninety seconds, or one and a half minutes.

Ling: Add the same amount of time to come back. That makes three minutes.

Carly: I swung on all the bars, like this.

Maggie: That's sixty seconds, or one minute. We're up to four minutes now.

Carly: Then I walked across the bridge, climbed the ladder, and went down the slide.

Maggie: Okay, let's time that.

Carly: Again? Oh, okay. That's one hundred and eighty seconds…

Sam: Or three minutes. Four plus three is only seven.

Carly: But I did it twice. Ask those kids if you want. Actually, I've done it three times now!

Peter: So we add another three minutes. That's ten minutes. Carly didn't take the cookies either!

Carly: Yeah, well, I did tell you that.

Peter: Maybe Maggie and Micky took them together... or Ling and Sam.

Micky: Why would I steal my own cookies?

Sam: And Ling would never lie!

Maggie: Hey, look at this **trail** of cookie crumbs on the ground!

Carly: Oh, yeah. Let's follow it.

Maggie: The cookie bag is right here!

Carly: And look who's next to it... George the dog from across the street – he got out of his yard again!

Everyone: Oh, George! It was you!

Peter: Oh, well. Sorry you guys missed out on the cookies. At least I had an energy bar!

Micky: I can't believe George ate all nine cookies!

Ling: Yeah. We could have given him the three that were left over.

Carly: I guess he wouldn't know that we would have had three left over.

Maggie: Well, he would if he knew his math!